20 Specs Needed To Buy The Right Dump Truck

Dr. Perry Jones Jr.

Dedication

THIS BOOK IS DEDICATED TO THE
HUSTLERS TURNED CEOS OUT THERE
WHO ARE DOING ALL THEY CAN TO
CHANGE THE FINANCIAL TRAJECTORY
OF THEIR FAMILIES FOR GENERATIONS
TO COME.

CONTENTS

Chapter

Chapter 1

Introduction

One of the biggest dilemmas in the world of dump trucking is to make sure that you have the right equipment to do the job adequately. This reality is not to be underestimated. The wrong equipment can be a costly mistake in several ways. First, it could cost you in lost jobs which may have to be forfeited due the inability to fulfill what a job requires. Secondly, it could cost you in major damage and breakdowns that occur from making a truck do what it is not capable of doing. Ultimately, using equipment in ways that it is not built to be used will result in lost work and ultimately send you out of business.

Finding the right truck is the second most asked question that I get about the dump truck business behind "how to find the work". This go-to guide will be helpful in getting the right specs for a dump truck. Finding the right truck is so vitally important and can determine your success or failure in this new business venture. Why do you need specs for a dump truck? Well, it's no different than buying a personal vehicle. You get what you need to perform at the level that you need.

Why am I so passionate about this? I made the grave mistake of buying a truck uninformed about the specs. In the year 2000 when I first started in the dump truck business, I purchased a 1994 Kenworth T800 Dump Truck. It had a new warren bed and was freshly painted. I was so enamored and big-eyed at the look that I didn't pay attention to more important things. First, this was a road truck conversion. That means that this truck was a road truck that was converted into a dump truck. Now the good news is that it was a Ryder fleet truck that was fleet maintained. They had maintenance records and an up-to-date dyno test (oil sample) so the truck was in great shape.

After purchasing this truck and bringing it home I still was oblivious to what was to come relating to the specs of the truck. Here are the specs. 1994 Kenworth Dump Truck, 12k front axle rating, 40k rear axle rating, 3:93 gear ratio, thin single frame, air ride suspension, and a basic dump bed. Immediately when I got my first load on the truck the suspension in the front went down on the front tires. This was because the 12k front axle rating is not enough for a triaxle dump truck. The air-ride road truck suspension was not beefed up enough to withstand the weight. I had to dump the load and set an appointment to get 2 leaf springs installed on each side of the front suspension. After this installation and $1500, this problem was solved. If I had gotten spring suspension this would have been no issue.

Soon after when hauling off road I soon begin to get stuck easily. The air-ride suspension began to be a problem. I was constantly getting pulled out which is not good for any truck. The pulling power just wasn't there with that 3:93 rear end ratio. All I could do was to install pull hooks and be cautious about what jobs I took which at times cost me money. Another facet of the air-ride suspension that was a problem is that I had to dump the bags when dumping to be safe. Finally, I had to cover the air bags to protect them from asphalt and other debris that could burst one of them. Again, if I had spring suspension this would be no problem. So, as you can see if I had been better, these issues would not have caused me problems at the beginning of my dump truck journey. Thank God, they didn't derail me from future success.

Chapter 2

Dump Truck Specs Part 1

So, what are some good specs for a dump truck that will insure you get a solid piece of equipment? What are some good pointers to look for to secure a good asset to invest in that will be good enough to make you plenty of money for years to come? In the following chapters, I will lay out for you what has worked for me after that first initial truck and continues to work for me today after 23 years.

When looking for a dump truck one of the first things I look for is what kind of suspension it has. If the suspension is not right or conducive for heavy hauling, I will no longer consider this truck as an option. The suspension is to a dump truck what a foundation is to a house. If the foundation is faulty, the rest of the truck will at some point have problems. When looking for specs on a truck suspension, I generally just want to make sure it's some type of spring suspension. Currently, my trucks have Camelback (Mack) Tuf Trac (Volvo & Western Star), and Haul Maax spring suspensions. (Internationals). Below is a picture of the Haul Maxx and T-Ride Suspensions.

Don't sleep or slip in this area. This issue is so important and will save you money coming into the business. While I do know some guys that bought tandems that were air-ride and and claimed they had no issues, the disclaimer is that those guys are doing mostly on-road hauling or house pads as a staple of their business. Tri-axle dump trucks and heavier trucks are just carrying too much weight to take a chance of going with an air-ride suspension.

The next spec for a dump truck under consideration is the frame. Much has been made of why the frame is important. The frame is the actual framework that sits on top of your suspension. The dump truck body sits on top of the frame. It has been the recommendation of many to go with a frame that is doubled. My first 15 to 20 trucks were all double framed. Why is this important? There have been instances where converted road trucks with a thin single frame began to bend right behind the cab of the truck. The weight of carrying a load instead of pulling a load began to take a toll on the suspension. Don't fool yourself. Over the course of time a frame can snap in half. I've seen trucks that this has happened to. These days they are making a thick single frame which is ok to get if a double frame is not available. The following picture is a thick single frame on one of my recent trucks that I purchased.

Please take this spec very seriously as it could cost you dearly in the long run. The cheap way out is not the cheap way out.

Our next spec is the front axle rating. This spec has to do with how much weight is recommended to be hauled on the front end of the truck. The axle weight rating can be found on the inside of the door panel of any commercial truck. The recommended front axle weight rating for a triaxle dump truck is 18,000 to 20,000 pounds. This axle weight rating will be sufficient to withstand the weight that will be hauled. I must reiterate that any weight less that this such as a road truck front axle weight rating will not be sufficient to haul consistently over time. I made this grave mistake and had to spend $1500 right out the door to beef up my front end so I could work. The following picture is a front axle on a dump truck.

Just as the front axle weight rating is important so is the rear axle weight rating. Dump trucks carry a lot of weight on top. Therefore, a dump truck must be made to carry the weight it will be carrying. The rear axle weight rating can also be found in the driver side door panel. The rear axle weight rating for a triaxle dump truck should be at least 44000 to 46000 pounds. This weight rating will be more than sufficient to adequately carry the weight that triaxles carry. The following picture is of a rear axle.

Do not forego any shortcuts to these critical weight ratings as they will determine whether your truck can haul what's being placed on it. Overloading a truck that can't handle the weight will cause expensive damage. A final word of note about these ratings. For quad and quint axles just simply modify your specs to be heavier for the added weight. Ex. My quad can carry 75,000 pounds legally in my state so my front axle rating is a little higher at 22,500 pounds, and my rear axle rating is 48,000 pounds.

The next spec up for consideration is the gear ratio. To give you a definition of this, the gear ratio is known as the ratio of rotation. Specifically, the gear ratio is the ratio of the number of teeth in the gear to the number of teeth in the pinion. The pinion is the smaller of the two gears. A gear with fewer teeth must rotate more times when it meshes with a gear that has more. For example, one of my recommended gear ratios is 4.11. If the ring gear has 37 teeth, and the pinion gear has 9 teeth, that would mean that for every one turn of the ring gear, the pinion will turn 4.11 times.

Why is this important? Ratios in the 4 range typically will allow for faster acceleration but lower the top speed. This ratio also will give the truck the torque and power needed for off road pulling but also decent speed while traveling on road. I've tried many combinations over the years and this one has worked the best for me. I'm in the swamps of Louisiana and the ground here in many cases is horrible. Additionally, the weight of triaxles and quad axles will in a day's time break even the hardest ground to pieces. Gears of the rear end are found inside the rear end housing on the following picture below.

Normally you will be able to get the spec sheet from a dealer to know the rear end gear ratio. If buying from a private owner and they don't know it, simply use the vin# and call the brand dealer and they can tell you.

Chapter 3

Dump Truck Specs Part 2

Our next spec is the asphalt apron. It is the bar at the bottom of the dump body below the tailgate. This spec is very important for those of us whose specialize in asphalt or wet batch concrete. While we refer to it as an asphalt apron this spec is very important when hauling other aggregates as well. This apron allows the material to fall out of the truck at a distance from the rear of the truck. As it is, material falls back under the truck and depending on what you are hauling can tear off a mudflap or damage a brake chamber. If your truck does not have an apron or you would like one, this can be fabricated at any welding and fabrication shop. The following picture below shows the asphalt apron.

The next dump truck spec is the high-lift tailgate. This invention from not long ago has been a God-send to the dump truck business. If you have been around for as long as I have (23 Years), then you know we didn't have this luxury for a long time. This new spec allows the driver to lift the gate up and into a position in which there is a bigger clearance for material to come out. This is especially great when hauling debris, rip rap, and broken concrete. The high-lift gate operates through air going to a set of cylinders that can be seen or unseen. The following picture below is a picture of the cylinders that operate the high lift tailgate.

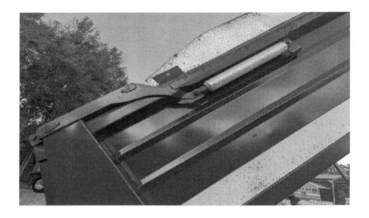

Most new trucks are coming with this spec already included as a part of the new dump body. However, if you are purchasing a new truck, don't assume. Be sure to ask the salesman if it has a high-lift gate. This feature helps to decrease wear and tear on the tailgate for years in the future.

Another spec you should look for in a dump truck is an automatic tarp. The days of winding a crank are over. An automatic tarp has several benefits. First, you won't have to leave the comfortable confines of your truck to roll the tarp back. Second, you will be free from weather concerns. Third, it saves times by allowing you to stay in the truck and move on to get another load. The following picture shows the tarp motor along with the arms from an electric tarp system.

Be sure to ask the salesman if there is an electric tarp system on the truck if you don't see it on the spec sheet. If you are talking to a private owner, you can simply ask them the question. Finally, if you are going to inspect the truck, be on the lookout for this spec. An additional word of note is that most dump trucks have a front to back tarp system, but occasionally you may run across a side to side system.

The next spec up for suggestion is to have a place on the truck to hold your diesel sprayer bottle/toolbox. This is an important thing to have especially for those who specialize in roadbuilding. This would suggest that you are hauling a whole bunch of asphalt and or wet batch concrete. When hauling this type of material preparation of the dump body is typically made by applying diesel or some type of other additive to make the material slide out freely from the dump body. Therefore, this additive is important to have with you on your truck.

There is a need to have a place to store the diesel sprayer preferably outside of the truck. Fumes from the diesel inside the cab can make one feel sick. The toolbox can house a small sprayer and hold needed tools for your dump truck. This type of platform can be fabricated by a fabrication shop or spec'd out when deciding what kind of dump bed you want on your truck. The following picture reveals a platform containing the diesel sprayer.

The last spec in this chapter is that of steerable axles. Some people refer to them as pusher axles. They get this name because when not in use they stay up but at the push of a button they come down and roll with the rest of your wheels. Dump trucks with three axles on the back (2 are the tandem that came originally with truck) are referred to as triaxles. The pusher axle makes the third axle. Four axles on back (2 pusher axles and the 2 tandems) are called quad axles. When observing this spec ask the question is the pusher axle a steerable axle. This means when you turn you don't have to raise the axle up at a stop sign, but instead you can keep rolling because the steerable axle will turn with the truck. This makes things much easier when operating your dump truck. Below is a picture of 2 steerable axles on one of my quad axles.

Chapter 4

Dump Truck Specs Part 3

The size of your dump body is of the upmost importance. First the size will determine how much material you will be able to legally carry on the highways. Typically for triaxles I look for 16–17-foot boxes with 3.5-to-4-foot sides. I really don't like the tall 4.5- and 5-foot sides and here is why. If you have a 20 cubic yard box and your buddy has an 18-yard box and you both are triaxles working hourly, then you are making the same thing, but you are carrying more thereby burning more fuel. Smaller dump bodies on triaxles works better for me since 99% of what I do is by the hour. You will have to determine if this works for you. The following is a picture of a steel dump body.

Second, I advocate for steel dump bodies and not aluminum. I do too much tear out of roads, thereby hauling broken concrete and asphalt to have an aluminum bed. It will simply not hold up to the wear and beating it would take hauling that kind of demotion material. Again, most of what I do is by the hour. Now if your context is such that the majority of what you do is by the load, and you are going to stay there then you might consider going the other route. Just know that the bed will not last over the course of time if it had to start hauling demolition material on a regular basis. My specs for my beds on a triaxle are 17 foot long and 3- 3.5 high. I try to get this whenever I can.

A particular spec that I have gotten regularly is to have construction lights or strobe lights. You may have noticed these as the lights on a dump truck that continually flash as you are operating the vehicle. There are several unique things related to these lights. First, you control whether they are on or off. They do not continually run so once you have left the construction site, you can turn them off. Second, you can get them in either red, white, or yellow. Lastly, I've found these lights to be very good for safety particularly at night alerting folks in cars that you are about to make some kind of move. The following is a picture of the location of a set of strobe lights on one of my trucks.

A shovel holder is an often-overlooked need of a dump trucker. For this spec I would suggest a place on the bed specifically designed to hold the shovel. In past time I have put it on the fuel tank, strapped them to the bed, and have even put them inside the truck with me. In later years I began to request a shovel holder come with the brand-new dump body or just simply get my welder to make something up for me. This item will make your job just that much easier. The picture below is the shovel and holder on one of my dump trucks.

The next spec has to do with safety. I wish I could say that every truck has this spec, but some don't. Make sure your dump body has some safety pins or stands for when you must prop bed up and work. Never assume that the bed will just stay up in the hold position. This is a sure-fire way for an accident to happen. I guarantee there will be a day when you will need to prop your bed and do some replacement of some sort or just to look around. Therefore, you will need to do this in a safe manner. The picture below is an example of some safety pins and where they go on one of my trucks.

The next spec has to do with the front tires on the triaxle dump trucks. Typically, you want to run a flotation tire on your truck. Currently, I run two different sizes of flotation tires. The sizes of these tires are as follows: 425/65/22.5, and 385/65/22.5. Take heed if you run a smaller tire. You may be reducing the amount of weight you can carry. I saw this happen here locally. Therefore, before you purchase a truck be sure to check this spec and see if they have the right size flotation. If not, maybe you can negotiate a deal to have them added. Here is a picture of the flotation tire being described.

Chapter 5

Dump Truck Specs Part 4

The next spec is one that is not talked about much at all. You will need to decide if you want a truck with a set forward or setback axle. This spec has some advantages depending on the type of work you do. The last two trucks that I bought at the time of this book were western stars with setback axles. I liked this spec because in doing road work the trucks are in neighborhoods and subdivisions. This allows them to make sharp right and left turns. The smaller turning radius also helps on construction sites when you must get in tight spots.

The set forward axle is the most popular of the two. It is also more common amongst construction trucks. The most common advantage is that it supports a longer wheelbase. I must say you can't go wrong with either one of these specs. It just all depends on what you like, and what kind of work you will be doing. I always try to get trucks that can be versatile. Here is a picture of both specs.

Another spec to consider when looking at purchasing a dump truck is what size fuel tanks you want to have. I bought my first truck which was a converted road truck (my mistake), and it had 125 gallon tanks on each side. This was good in that I could fuel up and run about 4 days sometimes 5. It was bad in that I had to spend a lot to fuel it up even in the year 2000. Now all my trucks pretty much range from a total of 100 to 150 gallons of fuel capacity. I've found this to be pretty good. We get about 2 to 3 shifts from a fill up depending on how we are running. Also, the bigger the tanks the more your empty and loaded weight will be. The below picture is the size of the tank on one of my trucks.

We are now moving on to our final set of specs. One of the much-needed specs for a dump truck is a pull hook(s). This allows the truck to be pulled out when you get stuck. Notice I said when you get stuck because in this business you are going to be stuck at some point. If you don't have any pull hooks on your truck, you will have to call a tow truck when you get stuck on jobs. Tow trucks are expensive to call upon when you need to be pulled out. Instead, if you have pull hooks a machine on the job can pull you out as well as another truck. These hooks also provide for safe pulling because trying to be pulled out with a load on you can damage your truck significantly. The picture below is an example of a pull hook.

The next spec is near and dear to my heart. It's the Allison automatic transmission. Years ago, when I heard of automatic transmissions in dump trucks, I thought people were crazy. Now that I've bought all automatics, I would not own anything else. Here are the benefits. The driver has to do no shifting and clutching. This allows a driver to not be as tired at the end of the day. This was enough for me when I first started driving the automatics.

Additionally, I found out that the pulling power is adequate even in off road conditions. I fully recommend the automatic in today's time also because there is no clutch to change or burn up. Finally, there are no gears being scratched when missing the shifting of the transmission. The below picture is the display of the controls for the Allison transmission.

Finally, the last spec for a good dump truck is the engine. Much has been suggested for the kind and size engine you should get. First, the size may surprise you. My first truck had a 350 N-14 Cummins in it. That was more than enough power to get the job done. When I moved to Mack, I upgraded to a 427 engine. This was the perfect combination of power and top end speed. 350 is enough horsepower to get the job done, but if you like a little more power then go for it.

The brand of the engine varies amongst people. It really boils down to your preference. Bottom line is they all need love and care to last. Currently, I have the following engines: Mack, Cummins, Detroit, and Volvo. I've had no problem out of any of these engines. Change the oil like you should and tend to the things it needs and you most likely won't have a problem. The picture below is of a Cummins engine in one of my trucks.

A final word on finding your dump. After you have observed all these specs, be sure to remember to ask for maintenance records. This will help you to see how the truck was taken care of. Be sure to ask if a dyno test has been done or if it is possible to be done. This will allow you to test the oil in the engine, transmission, and rear ends, which helps to determine if any metal or liquids are getting in that component.

Always go and look at the truck yourself. Nothing compares to the plain old eye test. In most instances you can tell if a truck has been well maintained. Take a mechanic with you to look over the truck and have him give you his opinion. Run the VIN number at the dealer and have them tell you what the truck had done to it. If it has gone to a dealer anywhere in the country, it will show up in the system.

Good luck and I wish you well in your endeavor to enter the dump truck business by purchasing a dump truck. Blessings to you and yours!

The Country CEO